Poems of Love and laughter

Gerald Spindel

ISBN: 0692329617
ISBN-13: 978-0692329610

THE UNVARNISHED PRESS
297 N. Frances St.
Sunnyvale, CA 94086
408-773-8711

To the women in my life, my friends and lovers:
To Sheila, my first and longest love;
To Connee, my late and great love.

Acknowledgment

To John McManus, whose encouragement, criticism, editing, and hard work made this book possible.

Contents

Part II: To Sheila

Part III: To Connee

Part One

Observations

A Father's Kiss

My father kissed me.
He woke me and he kissed me.
The year was 1943.
He was on his way to work.
I was leaving that morning for the Army.

My father didn't kiss me too often,
So I remember that kiss,
The scent of soap
On his freshly shaved face.
There were tears in his eyes
As he leaned over me
and kissed me,
His son going to war.
That was 1943.

Too soon, he was gone.
I never had the chance to say goodbye.
I love you Dad!

Memo to the Lost and Found

I lost my hat today.
I feel like such a fool.
It wouldn't be so hard to say,
But I've been to memory school.

I can memorize a shopping list
Or any of the yellow pages.
I remember the first girl I kissed
Though it really has been ages.

My G.I. serial number, say,
That really was a snap.
But I lost my hat today
And I feel like such a sap.

Pacific

My ocean is the Pacific.
Vast endless waters that I watch from the shore,
This shore at the end of land.
Waves form and break
Like an unending phalanx of warriors
Attacking the beach.

The endless wind from the west
Sculpts the wave-driven sand
Into series of musical notations
For a symphony in sand.

Would that I were a musician
Capable of reading that sculpted music.
Only the constant rush of the surf
Is the music that I hear.

Parking

I've forgotten where I parked my car
But I don't think I've come this far.
When I drove into this parking lot
The sun was high; the day was hot.
Now it's dark and to add to my pain
I feel it's beginning to rain.

Sure I've pushed the button, what do you think?
I'm just waiting for my darn car to blink.
I haven't seen anything blinking yet
But I am getting totally wet.

I've been wandering around seems half the night.
Wait! I see it! Over there on the right.
My good old blue Ford's blinking light.

Ants

I wish you'd tell me little ant
How you quickly appear where I think you can't.
There in the middle of the counter white
With ne'er an opening in my sight.
Suddenly I see you there
Walking on that surface bare.

Tell me ant, are you a scout?
Did the other anties send you out
To explore and see what you could learn
And bring back others on your return?

Say, little guy, you sure move fast,
But I'm afraid this trip will be your last.
For it's too bad, ant, you're going to linger
As I squash you with my index finger.

Air Terminal at Dawn

Outside: Flags of flame,
Rosy dawn against the pale blue sky.
Opposite the rising sun,
Fluffy pink clouds reflect the morning's glow.
Now the brown hills, rounded and seamed like old
leather
Have caught this rose of dawn
And shine with new light.

Within the terminal: Passengers reading,
Drinking coffee from paper cups.
Oblivious to the drama
Of a new day
Blazing in the windows behind them.

They check in, get seated, wait, wait,
While the flowing flags of dawn
Fade to the ordinary beauty
Of a new day.

The Lighted Window

What woke me from sleep I do not know.
It was two-thirty-one by my clock's fiery glow.
I turned and I tossed, kept trying to sleep,
But I just kept dozing and not very deep.
Now my clock showed three-twenty in digital red,
So I threw back the covers and left my bed.

I went to the window to look out at the night.
All was darkness except for one light.
One lighted window in a neighboring home
Broke the façade of darkness, one window alone.

Was another but me awake in the night,
Or had they forgotten to turn off the light?
Perhaps they rose early to go to work,
A policeman, a baker, a cook, or a clerk.
Could be two lovers hugging and kissing
Who want to see what in the dark they'd be
missing.

Maybe a parent with a child taken ill,
Or a compulsive reader who can't stop until
The whole book is finished and then go to bed.
As I watched, imagining these things in my head,
The light was extinguished and in darkness met
all the neighboring windows, and yet
I kept wondering what was behind that light
That I watched from my bedroom window at night.

The Backyard Tree

It was here when we moved in
Forty years ago.
Just a tree,
Fully grown to about twenty feet.
It didn't have the majesty of an oak,
The grace of an elm or a maple.
But its leafy branches gave us shade
And it sheltered birds
Within its welcoming arms.

Its presence was a gift
That we enjoyed extravagantly.
It required no care,
Fed only by sun and rain.
It was the perfect sentinel
To stand at our garden rear.
It would always be there.

And then one stormy winter night it fell.
We awoke in the morning
To see our tree, our sentinel,
Lay fallen across the width
Of our garden fence,
Its trunk down and branches
slumped in silent resignation.

Did it make a sound when it fell?
We were not awake to hear.
But if fell gracefully,
Slumped beside the fence
Within our own backyard.
Having spared the fence,
Was one last gift.

How long was it here
I do not know.
Trees do have years,
Lives that end as ours do.
Now when I look out the window
I see the fallen body of our tree,
Its branches, once reaching for the sky,
Now touching the earth.
Our tree is gone
And I know that I will miss it.

The Sorting Room

Let me tell 'bout the sorting room: we've lots and
lots of books.
There's History and Mystery and recipes for Cooks.
We've Romance and Medicine; they're both good
for your health.
Our Business/Economics books could add to your
wealth.

The Travel section's broadening, if that is to your
taste,
But Appearance will diminish if it happens at your
waist.
We have Art and we have Music, if culture's what
you're after.
And a section we call Humor; you'll double up with
laughter.

Anthologies are classified with English/Education.
In that same department, you'll find
Communication.
There's Religion for the pious and Psychology for
your Id,
Performance for the actor and Children's for your
kid.

Americana, California, Language and then
A place for Women's Issues, but nothing just for
men.
Anthropology and Nature, Classics old and new,
And we've Science Fiction for the futurist in you.

Occult and Serendipity, Lesbian and Gay,
Philosophy, Biography and books for Christmas Day.
Literature and Sociology both share a single aisle,
How-To and Recreation make your leisure time
worthwhile.

Reference and Science, Parenting and Ethnic too;
How about some Poetry for the romantic in you?
Math and Computers share a single section
And though we may complain, we regard all with
affection.

Many Happy Returns

My wife is returning a sweater that's black.
She thought it was blue when it hung on the rack.
A pair of shoes that she says are too tight.
When she tried them on, they fit her alright.
A couple of dresses that were very good buys;
When she got them home they weren't her size.

I think it's crazy, but she calls it shopping.
She gets so tired she just feels like dropping.
When she gets home and sees what she bought
And things don't fit as well as she thought,
We get into the car and return to the mall
Next thing I know, she's returning it all.

Eczema

"Eczema!" my doctor said.
Ex-Emma.
I didn't know Emma.
And now she was my ex.
I'm wrapped in her skin.
But if I had my choice,
I'd let her have it back,
Itch and all.

Reflected Truth

I walked past a mirror and what did I see?
A man staring back who looked a little like me.
A man somewhat older and much grayer too.
He had lots more wrinkles than the man that I
knew.

He had thinning hair and a larger midsection.
But the mirror can't lie; it's just a reflection.
So I accepted the fact and it wasn't so bad
Because it couldn't be me; it looked like my dad.

Pharmacy

Sing a song of pharmacy, a pocket full of pills.
Colors, shapes, and sizes meant to cure our ills.
A handful every morning, a mouthful in a throw,
Those colors shapes and sizes,
Hope they each know where to go.

Daisies

Look at me!
I am one of those people who live sanely and
sensibly.
Never go anywhere without
A thermometer, a hot water bottle, aspirin,
A raincoat and a parachute.

Careful and cautious, that's me.
Did I turn off the oven?
Did I lock the garage?
Just look at me!

If I had my life to live over
I would climb more mountains, swim more rivers,
Watch more sunsets.
I'd pick more daisies.

I would eat more ice cream and less spinach.
I would be crazier, more relaxed,
Less hygienic than I've been this trip.
And I'd pick more daisies.

I would dance the night away and walk barefoot on
the beach.
I'd go fishing on a river, skip pebbles on a stream,
And for sure, I'd pick more daisies.

I'd make love in the afternoon.
I'd make memories for a lifetime
And I'd give those daisies to my lover.

Part Two

To Sheila

The Post-War Dating Game

In 1946 Ben's uncle Henry was a patient at Mt. Sinai
Hospital
In mid-town Manhattan in New York City.
He had a nurse, Renée, he thought quite pretty.
Uncle said, "Renée, a girl so sweet,
I have a nephew I'd like you to meet."
"Okay," said Renée, "have him get in touch.
I would like to meet him very much."

The War ended in '45, the dating game
Was now alive with men who came
Back from overseas and all over the states
Ready to meet girls who were ready for dates.

So Ben called Renée as Uncle said
And this conversation led
To Ben telling Renée, "I have five pals."
To which Renée said, "I know gals.
Our nurses' residence has nine floors,
I think I can find five more."

This blind date was set for Saturday night.
Dates were assigned according to height.
Annette was the tallest so she got 6-foot-4 Stan,
Each girl to the appropriate man.
They said my date, Sheila, was a real cutie,
But she couldn't be there; she was on duty.

22

However, I had a substitute,
Her friend, Hannah, also cute.
Since I'd never met Sheila, it shouldn't matter at all
So I went with Hannah and we had a ball.

The following week I made up my mind
To look for Sheila and try to find
What I'd missed in the switch from Sheila to
Hannah.
I needed a number that I could call
My friend Stan collects numbers, he has them all.
Stan said, "On each floor there's only one phone
I have only one number, one number alone."

I said, "I'll give it a try just for fun.
You never can tell; it could be the right one."
So I dialed the number and waited while
It rang and rang. I couldn't help but smile.
A girl's voice answered, "Hello?"
I asked for Sheila, last name I don't know.
She said "We have Sheilas, at least four.
Maybe you can tell me more."

I said, "Sheila was on duty Saturday late
And had to miss a mass blind date."
"Oh," she said, "That was Sheila Axelrad. Wait, I'll
get her."
That indeed was Sheila and how I met her.

Blind Date

Discharged from the Army and the company of
men,
In 1946 I was a civilian once again.
Twenty-one-years-old, I had just one goal in mind,
That was to meet the nicest girl I could find.

So when I was offered the chance for a blind date
With a student nurse named Sheila, I could hardly
wait.
I met her at the nurses' residence hall,
A lovely young woman, brunette and tall.
Her eyes were so blue, her smile so bright,
I knew we would have a fabulous night.

We went to an outdoor concert and sat on a bench
for two.
The music that night was Rhapsody in Blue.
She was listening intently, so I got bolder
And put my arm across her shoulder.
She moved away!
I heard myself say:
"Where are you going?" My ego was breaking.
"It's okay," she said "I'm not taking
Up all that much room.
Besides, we'll be leaving soon."

We got back to the hall without any talk.
I vowed never again to be out for a walk
Or a date with this cold miss.
I certainly didn't want -- or get -- a goodnight kiss.

A week later my friend Stan had a student nurse
date.
He said, "Ask Sheila." But I said "Wait!
Asking Sheila is only looking for trouble."
He sighed: "My date only goes double.
Come on, you might have been wrong
You and Sheila might still get along."

So I went on the date with Sheila once more
But this date didn't turn out like the one before.
We went to a dance
It was my second chance.
This wasn't really love at first sight.
But looking back it turned out all right.
When Sheila graduated as a nurse
I asked her to marry me for better or worse.
She and I were wed in New York on November 21,
1948
And we both laughed remembering our blind date.

You Pack!

Life in Long Island suburbs, two kids and two cars,
A mortgage, neighbors and a lawn needing cuts,
Blazing hot summers and snow up to our butts.
Shoveling snow was no joke,
Not a job for us city folk.

I said to Sheila, "Let's get away from this strife.
I can't do this for the rest of my life.
No parents to hold us, we're all on our own.
The decision we make is ours alone."
"You're right," said Sheila, "you know what we lack.
So since you've convinced me, how about you pack?"

Then I asked Sheila, "Where should we go?"
"Wherever we go," she replied, "let's have no snow.
California sounds okay,
Let's go that way.
I'm tired of this suburban whirl;
You know that I'm a city girl."
"So let's go to a city, is there one around?
There's San Francisco. How does that sound?"
"Sounds good to me. I've never been there.
People will mumble, but what do we care."

That was December with snow on the ground
And I saved all of the cartons I found.
Cartons and barrels and boxes and cases,
All that I found in various places.
We packed some chairs and some tables
Clothes and linens in boxes with labels.
We sold the house and then that night,
I said to Sheila, "Are you nervous? Are we doing
right?"
She said "I love you. I know we'll succeed.
We have the boys and each other
What more do we need?"

We got into our car, a Dodge wagon of blue,
And headed west on an adventure that was new.
Twelve days of driving across the nation.
We finally reached our destination,
Over the bridge across the bay
To San Francisco and here we'll stay.
First we joined a congregation
And enjoyed participation
With the people we met
And never felt regret
For the choice that we made way back
When Sheila said, "You pack."

Losses

When did it start?
Did it start when you
Forgot how to use
Our washing machine?
How to drive our car?

Or was it further back than that?
When your handwriting
Became illegible?
We joked about that:
Maybe you should become a doctor.
Their handwriting is illegible.
We all laughed.

But the little losses
Were adding up.
What month, what day,
What year is this?
You couldn't sign your name.
You didn't recognize your sons.

Little losses, Alzheimer's losses
Stealing your mind.
Stealing you away
From your family, from yourself,
From me.

Ghost Voices

I loved to see her sweet face across the table.
She had a smile that could banish gloom.
Angry words may have passed between us during
the day,
But there was always love
And we kissed good night in bed.

She used to call out to me when the garage door
closed:
"Honey, is that you?"
That was when there were children at home.
But our sons are grown and gone.
Gone to children of their own.
"Honey is that you?"

And when I was late coming from a meeting,
She came halfway down the stairs
And watched me drive into the garage.
"I was waiting for you. I missed you."
And when I looked at her sweet smiling face
I knew that I was a lucky man.
"I am waiting for you. I miss you."

Now I hear a ghost voice
From past that is still present.
"Honey is that you?"
Something has been stolen from me.

Alzheimer's disease, that evil thief,
Has taken your mind and left your body intact.

Now when I come home there is no one waiting,
Only ghost voices.
You live someplace else and I visit you there.
Do you know me? My darling, my wife, my love?
I am waiting for you, I miss you.

I Know You Can't Read This

I just wanted you to know
That you made my life complete.
That every day was brighter
Because of you.

Every ordinary day
From breakfast to bed was special
Because you were my wife.

Our home was a joy
Because of you.
You gave me strength
when I needed strength.
You gave me courage
When I doubted my own.
I love you very much.
I just wanted you to know.

Now our home is empty
Without you.
When I see you,
You don't know who I am.

I still have the strength
and courage you gave me
Or I couldn't manage
Without you.

Your mind is an Alzheimer's tangle,
But I remember who you were
And I still love you very much.
I know that you can't read this
But I just wanted you to know.

Sheila's Smile

I remember your smile,
How your eyes, your face lit up.
Like sunrise,
Your smile lighted the world for me.

But you don't smile any more.
Oh, once in a while I can
Make you give the briefest lip curve.
That will have to do.
But you don't smile anymore
For me or for anyone.

There is nothing to smile about now.
You are lost,
Lost with a brain that's tangled
Like steel wool.
I have to accept. I can't bring you back.
I have lost your smile.
I have lost you, my beloved, I have lost you.

This Isn't You

This person sitting here starring blankly at nothing,
This isn't you.
This angry person calling me names:
"Stupid botch!" "Stinking clump!"
This isn't you.

Confused, lost language
Groping for words, now only syllables.
Diapered, like a large child.
Struggling with fork and spoon
To feed yourself.
Not remembering your own sons.
No, this isn't you.

You are the woman in the picture,
The woman in the pink dress
With the bright smile
Standing beside me
In the photo.

You are the woman in my arms,
The woman I love,
Bright, funny, wise.
The woman in my memory.
That was you.

I grieve for the woman I have lost.
I must accept the woman you are.
I still love you.
But this isn't you
Yet it is.

Journeys

Now you are free.
Freed of the tubes and wires
That had tethered you
To the bottles and bags
That fed you,
To the machine
That monitored every beat
Of your loving heart,
Your blood, your breath.

You are free.
Only the blissful cloak of morphine
To gentle your way,
Your sorrowful journey
To eternity.

Now we are alone,
Alone with the memories
Of the wonderful woman
We knew and loved.
Oh, the dreadful decision
To let you go!

To free you from the pain
And the deadening darkness
That kept you from us.
Now you are free,
Free to fall all the way,
And ours is the sorrowful journey
As we watch you go.

Remains

Your toothbrush is still here
And your comb, your mirror,
They're here too.
Right where you left them.

Your dresses and shoes,
Dressy high-heel patent,
You'll never use them again.
The cowboy shirt
That you ordered
From a catalog
And you wore only once.
That's here too.

They're all waiting
For you.
But you're not coming back.
Things, lots of things
That make a life remain
After the living is through,
After you have been taken
From me.

To Sheila

What is sorrow
When I think of the joy
That I had with you?
Today I mourn
But when I reflect on the years
That we shared
I will celebrate
The wonderful days
That were ours.
What a stroke of good fortune
To have had
You, Sheila, for my wife.

Part Three

To Connee

Once Again

I was seventy years old
When I fell in love
For the second time,
Or maybe the third or fourth.

The first two didn't count.
They were the flush of youth
Joined when war
Made uncertain tomorrows
And faded in the blaze of peace.

Now I have lost
The one true love in all my life.
The girl I married,
The woman, my wife
I love with all my
Heart and soul
I have lost.
Alzheimer's, this cruel disease,
Has taken her from me.

And now that I've met you,
Am I free to love again?
Am I free, truly free in my heart?
Oh, my new love
What can I say to you?

How can I tell you
That I love you
When I love another woman
Who still lives
But is lost in a mental tangle?
I am one man and I love both women.

Revelation

I never thought I could love again;
The hurt was too real, too new.
When I met you there was something,
But I was afraid and I ran away.

I never thought I could love again,
Until I let myself know you
Know the sweetness, the caring person
Behind those green eyes, behind the bright smile.

Now I know you, Connee.
I know the joy that you have brought to me
And I hope that I have brought to you.
I love you, truly I do.

When we do things together,
Cook, dance, talk,
Make love,
It's wonderful.

You make me feel
Like a hero, young and strong
Because you are my love.

Tashlich

Tashlich is a ritual where we cast away sins.
It's a custom we follow as the new year begins.
We head for the ocean and there at the beach
We throw all our sins far out of reach.

Then we return with a slate free and clear
All ready to start fresh in the new year.
And if we should happen to sin some more,
We'll go back to the ocean as we did before.

But it's really no sin when we feel as we do
And it's wonderful when I make love to you.
So we'll treat Tashlich as a ritual event
Because I'm sure that for us it's not meant.

Western Windows

When I speak to you at morning,
The dawn is breaking.
Light comes into my home,
And your voice on the phone
Brings joy into my heart.
You make my day begin.

Then I speak to you at evening.
We watch the sunset together
Over the telephone.
And we share the pleasure,
The colors, the changing sky.
How you make my heart sing!

Ah, but when I hold you
And there is no phone,
There's only you and me.
Then I kiss you and I feel the thrill
That I always feel when I'm with you.
My heart sings and dances with new life.

Even In the Vast Desert of Sorrow

You brought laughter to my life.
You showed me that joy can be found
Even in the vast desert of sorrow.

You are living proof
That youth has nothing to do with age.
Now you are seventy and, safe to say,
That when people heard the news
They wondered what kind of calendar you use.
Because, and this is honest truth,
Your attitude is really one of youth.

So as we celebrate this happy day,
We say, "Please always stay this way."

A Package of Gifts

I bring you a package of gifts:
I give you two arms to hold you so tight.
Two smiling eyes day or by night.
Two lips to kiss yours and feel the thrill.
A heart that loves you and always will.

Body and soul, I'm yours for all time.
Your gift to me is "I'm so glad that you're mine."

Can You Abide Me?

Watcher of sunsets,
Walker of dawn,
Lover of moonlight,
Can you abide me?
A dreamer of dreams,
Writer of words,
Fixer of things broken.

Come live with me
My love is for you
Only, only for you.

We'll walk dawns together,
Watch sunsets together,
Dream dreams together,
And make love by moonlight.

The Answer

I'm glad you said "Yes"
When you could have said "Wait."
You could have said "No,
No, it's much too late.

"I'm seventy-one and you're seventy-two.
It's much too late to marry
At this stage of our lives.
What will people say?
What will our children think?"

But you didn't say "No."
You didn't say "Wait."
Instead you said "Let's go,
Let's give it a whirl,
I'm seventy-one but
I feel like a girl"

That's what love can do
For me and for you.
I love you more today
Than I did back then.
And if you ask me now,
I'd do it again.

After the Wedding

Connee, my darling,
Now as we start a new life
Together as husband and wife
Let us take this love that we have found,
Nurture it and feed it.
As you would the flowers that you grow,
We'll see our love blossom and grow.

We have both known the bleak winter of sorrow.
Now, in the springtime of our love,
We'll know new life.
How I look forward to the joys we will share.
I love you, Connee, Connee, my wife.

Second Chance

When I was young and fancy free
I married my love at twenty-three.
She was my darling, beloved wife.
We would be together for all of life.
But her life has ended and I still live
And I have so much more love to give.

I thought I was finished at seventy-two
That's what I thought until I met you.
Now I'm in love all over again.
I consider myself the luckiest of men.
To have you and a whole new life
With you my darling, my wonderful wife.

To Connee, After Surgery

I walked this morning, as I usually do.
The sea wind was brisk and quite cold.
Walking, I kept thinking of you
And how you make me feel young and so bold.

I thought my romantic life was over;
I'd never know real intimacy again.
And now with you I've become a lover
With more joy than I can't remember when.

Until you come home, I'll have to wait
Till I hold you in my arms once more.
I'll give you time to recuperate
Before we live our lives as before.

Post-Op

I'm thankful for your successful operation.
Now comes time for recuperation.
Later we can think of recreation,
When you've improved your situation.

But I can tell you without hesitation,
I'm looking forward to your rehabilitation
And await with great anticipation
To greet you with a large osculation.

If I Were An Artist

If I were an artist,
I'd pick up my paint
And put you on canvas.
But an artist I ain't.

If I could write music,
I'd write you a song.
But that's one more place
Where my talent's not strong.

If I were a sculptor,
I'd form you in clay.
But your flesh is much nicer.
And I prefer you this way.

Perhaps as a poet
I can tell you in rhyme
Of how much I love you
And can't wait for the time

When I hold you and kiss you
And love you once more.
You know how I miss you.
My darling, it's you I adore.

An Ageless Lover

At my age I've become a great lover.
I have to believe that it's true
You've said it so many times over.
But it's because I make love to you.

Whenever I see you I want you.
When I hold you I can't let you go.
I thrill whenever you touch me.
These are things that I want you to know.

To my life you brought love and laughter
When I thought love had gone for good.
You brought spice to my life after
You taught me to love spice in food.

I want to hold you in my arms and kiss you.
It can be both by night and day.
That will be my way to wish you
A very loving and happy birthday

Love by Lightning

Awake in the darkness,
We heard the distant grumble of thunder
And I held you close
While lightning flashed in the night.

Toothpasty kisses in the darkness,
I caressed your sleep-warm body
While the night outside crackled with fire
And we made love by lightning.

The sounds of your pleasure thrilled me
And then your pleasure became my own
As our lips met in love
By lightning in the night.

My Poem is You

Happy birthday, my Connee,
My darling, my love.
My poem is you.
You set me in rhyme.
You came into my life
At just the right time.

To say how I love you
Is hardly enough
To show how I feel
About you.
You are my song
You are my joy
My darling, my sweetheart
My love and my life.

Happy birthday my dearest
Connee, beloved of mine.
I would give you my heart,
But you have it now.

The Gift

I looked at my calendar this afternoon
And there was your birthday coming up soon.
I want to give you a nice present,
One both expensive and pleasant.

My first thought was jewelry -- diamonds and gold.
But those things are so common and so cold.
What can I get you that's unique with plenty of
charm,
A gift you'll enjoy, one you can hold in your arms?

And right then I had an inspiration!
There's no need for mental agitation,
Because I have the perfect gift,
One that I think will give you a lift.

You may have guessed what the gift would be
Because this gift for you is also for me.
We'll share it together as I intend it.
It's the perfect gift, but how do I send it?

I'll just deliver it in person.

The Slim Firmness of You

My lover, my friend,
You mean so much to me.
To hold you and kiss you,
To feel the slim firmness of you,
Of your sweet body in my arms
Makes my own body thrill
And respond with pleasure.
Making love to you is sheer joy.

Watcher of sunsets,
Cooker of soups,
My kitchen companion,
You are always in my heart.
My smiling, laughing lover,
My sweet, understanding,
Passionate and compassionate lover.

Happy birthday, my love.
You grow younger every year.

To Connee

I found your earrings on my dresser this morning.
I watched as you stood by the mirror
And you removed them from your ears.
How you tilted your head
Used both hands to slip each one
From your pretty pierced ears.
How feminine your movements,
So graceful.

I caught your eye in the mirror
And you smiled,
And you came to me,
And I held you in my arms.

Watcher of Sunsets

Watcher of sunsets,
Walker of dawn,
Lover by moonlight.

I watch your calm face
In the lamplight
Eyes downcast,
Concentrating on your reading.
How that calm belies
The passion in you
That I know,
That I have shared.

My lover by moonlight,
Lover by dawn,
Watcher of sunsets.
Your white hair,
Your six dozen kind years
Can't be true.
No, not a woman
As young, as exciting as you.
In love,
And much beloved
By me.

We Had it All

I thought it could never end.
Our love, our life together
Would go on forever.
But forever is a long, long time
And now it's over.
My bed is lonely
My arms are empty with loss.

Once, we had it all.
The joy of our love
Made every day a new adventure.
To wake with you at my side,
To know that you were there
In my world, in my life,
Made laughter in my heart.

I've Been Here Before

I've cried here and I've laughed here too.
So why have I come back?
Back to this house of memory,
of sorrow and of joy?

I've come back because
I don't want to be alone.
I want to reach out to others like me,
People who know what it's like
To care for a loved one
When there is no hope,
Knowing that love will make
the difference.

Yes, I've been here before
And each time it made a difference.
Maybe this time it will make
a difference for you, too.

Night Love

My clock says 3:30 AM.
So what am I doing sitting at my desk
At 3:30 AM and writing poetry?
Writing poetry and thinking of you.

I think of you and my empty arms
ache to be holding you.
Even at 3:30 AM your kisses
Made these small hours so sweet.

In the gray light before dawn
Or in the lightning-pierced darkness,
you came into my arms
And we held back the night with love.

So I sit here at my desk writing.
The dark and silent world outside
Waits for the daylight while I have
Only my memories of you, your kisses,
And our love.

Late Love

Late love, great love.
Second wife, second life.
To love again, to live again.
To live and to lose;
To lose once more.
The pain is as great
As the pain before.

About the Author

Gerald Spindel has been scribbling verse since he was eight, in 1933. He was born and raised in New York City, graduating from De Witt Clinton High School in 1942. He served in the Army Air Corps from 1943-46, as an aerial gunnery instructor. After the war, he enlisted as a student at NYU and Columbia University, but dropped out of both. He tried his hand at script writing, accumulating a small pile of rejection slips. In 1962, he packed up his wife and two young sons and drove west until he hit the Pacific. He became a successful salesman in San Francisco, a city he loves. He lost both of his wives to complications of Alzheimer's disease.